THE
SALMON AND TROUT
RECIPE BOOK

Compiled and published by
Geerings of Ashford Ltd.

Illustrations by Barbara Seth.

ISBN 1 873953 15 1

Designed and printed by Geerings of Ashford Ltd.,
Cobbs Wood House, Chart Road, Ashford, Kent. TN23 1EP

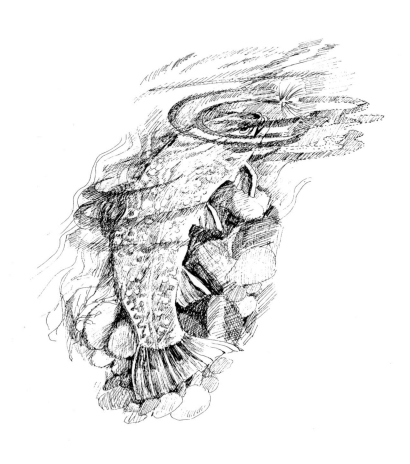

CONTENTS

FOREWORD

This collection of recipes focuses on Salmon and Trout, fish that have a special appeal, both in the water and on the plate.

In the river, catching a Salmon or a Trout demands skill and patience such that success is a triumph of techniques and persistence, always worthy of celebration. Where better to celebrate than in the kitchen, where both are so welcome? Their distinctive flavours and texture, neither bland nor overwhelming, make them immensely versatile, whether simply grilled or complemented by a wonderful range of imaginative sauces.

Although trout and salmon have humble beginnings when, in centuries past, both were considered food for the masses, they have enjoyed a luxury status for many years, gracing the menu in only the grandest of hotels and restaurants and the tables of only the priviledged and the poacher. However, in recent years modern farming methods have put both on the table as never before. Of course, this has led to a heated debate as to the relative merits of "farmed" or natural fish but I for one cannot tell the difference although the fish I catch myself taste just that little "sweeter".

So whether your fish are from the river, "farmgate" fresh or via your local supermarket, you'll find this collection of recipes an essential guide to the culinary delights of salmon and trout.

Tight lines and bon apetite.

PHILIP WHITE
Head River Keeper to the Duke of Rutland in Derbyshire and author on fly fishing and fly dressing.

SALMON STARTERS

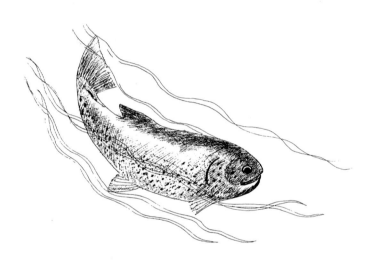

MARINATED FISH WITH CHILLI AND GREEN PEPPER

(serves 4)

6oz/185g salmon fillet, skinned and boned
6oz/185g fresh tuna or monkfish, skinned and boned
Olive oil for brushing

Marinade:
Thinly pared rind and juice of 1 lime
4 tablespoons/60ml olive oil
1 small red chilli (seeded and thinly sliced in rings)
Salt and pepper

To serve:
1 small green pepper (halved, seeded and diced)
1 tablespoon chopped coriander
Coriander sprigs to garnish

Remove all bones from the fish. Brush a frying pan with a little olive oil, place over a high heat until smoking, add the fish to the pan and cook for 20 seconds on each side. The pan should be very hot to seal the fish on the outside only without cooking the inside. Remove the fish from the pan and cool completely. Make the marinade in a shallow dish mixing the lime rind, juice and olive oil and adding the red chilli and salt and pepper to taste.

Cut the fish into thin strips or chunks, add to the marinade and toss carefully until mixed. Cover and leave to marinate in the refrigerator for 1 hour.

Take the fish out of the marinade, arrange on individual serving dishes and add the coriander. Sprinkle the green pepper over the fish and spoon a little of the marinade over the dish to serve.

SMOKED SALMON PARCELS
(serves 4)

3 sheets filo pastry (thawed if frozen)
Melted butter for brushing

Filling:
6oz/185g smoked salmon (diced)
12oz/350g ricotta or curd cheese
2 tablespoons chopped chives or dill
Pinch of ground nutmeg
Salt and pepper

Dill butter sauce:
1 shallot (finely chopped)
3 tablespoons/45ml white wine vinegar
3 tablespoons/45ml water
8oz/250g unsalted butter (chilled and cubed)
Squeeze of lemon juice
2 tablespoons chopped dill or fennel

To garnish:
Dill or fennel sprigs

Set oven 200°C/400°F/Gas Mark 6.

To make the filling, mix together the salmon, ricotta or curd cheese, herbs, nutmeg and seasoning until smooth. Cut the filo pastry into twelve to sixteen 4"/10cm squares, brush with melted butter and place a spoonful of salmon filling in the middle of each square. Draw the pastry up around the filling, pinching to form a parcel shape and arrange the tops attractively. Place salmon parcels on a greased baking tray, brush with melted butter and bake in the oven for 10-15 minutes until golden.

While parcels are cooking make the dill butter sauce. Put the shallot, vinegar and water in a small pan, bring to the boil and cook steadily until reduced to about 2 tablespoons/30ml. Reduce heat and gradually whisk the butter in lightly a piece at a time until creamy and smooth; this process should not take long. Do not allow to boil or the sauce will separate. Stir in the chosen herbs and seasoning.

Arrange the cooked parcels on individual serving plates, attaching a herb sprig around each one and spoon a little sauce around them. Serve immediately.

SALMON & CUCUMBER STARTER
(serves 4)

1lb/450g boned salmon (skinned)
Finely grated rind and juice of 1 lime
Half ounce/15g sugar
Salt and pepper
Half cucumber (unpeeled and finely grated)
1 teaspoon tarragon or herb mustard
1-2 tablespoons/15-30ml thick sour cream
1 tablespoon chopped dill

To garnish:
Herb sprigs
Lime slices

Lightly oil four 4fl.ozs/125ml ramekin dishes or individual moulds. Carefully remove all bones from the salmon and place in a shallow dish. In a small bowl mix the lime rind and juice with the sugar and 1 tablespoon of salt and rub mixture into the salmon. Cover and leave to marinate in the refrigerator for at least 4 hours, turning once.

Sprinkle the cucumber with 1 tablespoon salt, toss gently, transfer to a colander and leave to drain for 30 minutes.

In a bowl, mix the mustard, sour cream, chopped dill and seasoning. Take the salmon out of the marinade and pat dry. Cut fish into small pieces and add to the mixture. Rinse the cucumber, pat dry and add to the fish mixture, mixing well. Put into the prepared dishes or moulds and leave to chill for at least one hour.

To serve, turn out on to small plates and decorate with herb sprig and lime slices. Delicious served with black rye bread or pumpernickel.

STRIPED FISH TERRINE
(serves 4-6)

12oz/350g boned salmon (skinned)
1 egg white
5fl.oz/150ml double cream
Lemon juice to taste
Salt and pepper
12oz/350g sole fillets (skinned)

Cut salmon into 1"/2.5cm pieces, place in a blender or food processor and purée until smooth adding the egg white and blending again until evenly mixed. Put in the refrigerator and chill for at least 30 minutes. Return mixture to the blender or food processor and add the cream, lemon juice and seasoning, blending until smooth. Chill for 30 minutes.

Cut the sole fillets into long strips and roll in the chopped herbs until well coated. Set the oven at 180°C/350°F/Gas Mark 4.

Grease a 1lb/450g loaf tin or terrine with butter. Spoon one third of the chilled salmon mixture into the tin, spreading evenly, and lay the herbed sole strips on top, leaving a border at each side. Carefully spoon the remaining salmon mixture over the sole. Smooth evenly and level the surface. Cover with buttered foil and place in a roasting tin, containing enough hot water to come half-way up the sides of the loaf tin/terrine. Bake in the oven for 35 minutes or until a skewer inserted into the centre comes out clean.

Lift the terrine out of the roasting tin and leave until cold. Remove the foil, cover with oiled greaseproof paper and weight down. Chill for at least 4 hours before carefully turning out. Cut into slices, garnish with mustard and cress and serve with creme fraiche.

SMOKED SALMON MOUSSE
(serves 6)

10oz/275g smoked salmon
Half a chicken stock cube
2 teaspoon gelatine
4 tablespoons/60ml water
6fl.oz/150ml single cream
2 tablespoons/30ml lemon juice
Freshly ground black pepper
Freshly grated nutmeg
10fl.oz/250ml double cream (whipped)
2 egg whites
Parsley and/or lemon slices to garnish
6 ramekin dishes

Put water, stock cube and gelatine in a small pan and place on a very low heat to dissolve. Put the salmon in a food processor or liquidizer and whiz, add the single cream, lemon juice, pepper and nutmeg and briefly whiz again. Pour mixture into a bowl and stir in the dissolved gelatine. Fold in the whipped cream. Whisk the egg whites until they are very stiff and, using a metal spoon, fold in quickly but thoroughly into the smoked salmon mixture. Divide mixture evenly between the ramekin dishes and leave in a cool place to set. When ready to serve garnish with chopped parsley and/or thin slices of lemon.

SALMON MOUSSE

12oz/300g salmon (cooked, skinned and boned)
3oz/75g creamed butter
6 tablespoons/90ml cool white sauce (see page 107)
2 tablespoons/30ml sherry, Madeira or white wine
2 tablespoons/30ml cream
Salt and pepper

Garnish:
Half pint/250ml fish aspic
A few thin cucumber slices, peeled sliced tomato and sprigs of parsley or tarragon

Place salmon in basin with butter and Béchamel sauce and pound well, adding sherry, Madeira or wine. Then add cream and seasoning to taste. Turn mixture into a dish and allow to cool. Cover with a thin layer of aspic which is cool but not quite set and dip the garnishes in the remaining aspic and place on top of the mousse. Set aside to cool. Finally fill the rest of the dish with the remaining aspic which is cool but not set.

SALMON SOUP
(serves 4-6)

1 salmon head and bones
1lb/450g raw fish bones and trimmings
1 leek (chopped)
1 stalk celery (chopped)
1 large onion (skinned and chopped)
1 clove garlic
2 teaspsoons salt
12 peppercorns
1 bay leaf
Bunch of parsley with stalks
3 pints/1.3litres water
2 tablespoons/30ml olive oil
1 onion (chopped)
3 white parts of leeks (chopped)
3 large tomatoes (skinned and chopped)
Half pint/250ml white wine

To make your fish stock, place the first 11 ingredients in a large saucepan and boil for about 30 minutes. Then strain and set aside.

Heat olive oil in saucepan and lightly fry onion and leeks adding tomatoes, wine and fish stock. Cook for 20 minutes and then add salt and pepper to taste. Just before serving add any leftover flakes of salmon.

Alternatively, add 1 tablespoon of grated parmesan cheese, 4 tablespoons of thick cream and 1 small tin of salmon to the soup.

SALMON IN ASPIC JELLY
(serves 4)

12ozs/350g cooked salmon (roughly flaked)
5fl.ozs/125ml sparkling white wine
1 small cucumber
1 pkt aspic (crystals)
1 tablespoon finely chopped parsley
Small bunch of watercress

Arrange flaked salmon in the base of a lightly oiled ring mould and scatter over the chopped parsley. Dissolve the aspic in three-quarters pint of hot water, stirring until the crystals are dissolved and add the wine. Pour into the mould until it reaches the top and pour remainder on to a shallow plate. Leave it to set. When ready to serve, loosen sides of mould with a knife and carefully invert onto a serving dish. Chop the remainder of the aspic jelly with a wet knife and fill the centre of the ring. Garnish with washed watercress and arrange thinly sliced cucumber round the edge. Serve immediately.

SMOKED SALMON PATÉ
(serves 4)

8ozs/225g smoked salmon trimmings (cut into small pieces)
1oz/25g unsalted butter (softened)
1 tablespoon/15ml dry sherry
1 tablespoon/15ml lemon juice
Pepper
6 tablespoons/90ml double cream

Put salmon pieces, butter, sherry and lemon juice into liquidiser and blend until smooth. Season to taste with pepper, add the cream and continue to blend long enough to mix the ingredients. Spoon into serving dishes and chill.

Serve with hot toast and lemon wedges or spread on small biscuits to serve with drinks.

POTTED SALMON

Equal quantities of salmon (cooked, boned and skinned) and soft butter
A little white pepper
A little white wine or lemon juice
A pinch of nutmeg
Melted clarified butter

Put all the ingredients into a bowl and pound well together, adding only enough wine or lemon juice to make the consistency soft and even. Test for seasoning and put in small pots. Put aside to cool and then cover with a layer of cooled clarified butter. Keep in refrigerator until ready to serve.

SALMON AND PARSLEY SOUP
(serves 6-8)

6oz/175g cooked salmon (bones and skin removed and flaked)
2oz/50g butter
1 large onion (skinned and chopped)
2 large potatoes (peeled and finely chopped)
1 pint/550ml chicken stock
1 pint/550ml milk
Freshly grated nutmeg
Salt and black pepper
2 tablespoons chopped parsley

Put the butter in a pan and melt over a moderate heat. Add the onion and cook for about 5 minutes until soft and transparent. Add the potato and cook for a further two minutes. Pour in the stock and milk and add nutmeg and salt and pepper to taste. Cover the pan and allow mixture to simmer gently for half an hour or until the potato is soft, stirring occasionally. Remove pan from heat and allow to cool. Put mixture through a blender or food processor with the parsley until smooth and add the flaked salmon. Reheat thoroughly to serve but not for too long as the parsley will discolour.

SALMON WITH ORANGE AND WALNUTS
(serves 6)

5oz/150g butter
Half teaspoon salt
3oz/75g broken walnuts
12oz/350g cooked salmon (skin and bone removed and flaked)
Grated rind of 1 large or 2 small oranges
Juice of 1 lemon
Freshly ground black pepper
Pinch grated nutmeg

Melt butter in a saucepan and pour into a bowl leaving about 2 tablespoons/30ml in the pan. Add the salt and walnuts and stirring occasionally, fry walnuts on a moderate heat for about 5 minutes. Tip onto a good thickness of kitchen paper to absorb excess fat.

Put the flaked salmon in a food processor, add the grated orange rind and blend. Add the lemon juice and blend again. Slowly add the cooled, melted butter until all is blended into a smooth purée. Season with the nutmeg and black pepper. Stir in the walnuts – do not use the food processor or you will lose the "nuttiness" of the walnuts. Put mixture into a large serving dish or six small dishes and serve with brown bread or toast.

SMOKED SALMON MOUSSE WITH CHIVES
(serves 4)

4oz/125g smoked salmon
6oz/175g cream cheese
7fl.oz/200ml single cream
1-2 tablespoons/15-30ml lemon juice
Salt & fresh ground black pepper
Grated nutmeg
1 teaspoon/5ml gelatine
4 tablespoons snipped chives
1 egg white
Chives and lemon wedges to garnish
4 ramekin dishes

Cut eight strips from the smoked salmon 3"x¹/₄"/7.5cmx6mm and set aside. Keep a few more small strips rolled up and also set aside for garnishing. Chop up the remaining salmon. Beat the cheese and cream together, add the lemon juice and nutmeg and season with the salt and pepper.

Put 4 tablespoons/60ml water in a small jug, sprinkle the gelatine over and leave to soak for a few minutes. Place jug in a pan of hot water to melt the gelatine mixture or microwave on high for 30-45 seconds, then stir into the cheese mixture. Add the chives and chopped salmon and mix thoroughly. Set mixture aside in a cool place, stirring occasionally until just beginning to set. Whisk the egg whites until soft peaks form and fold carefully into the cheese mixture.

Place two strips of the salmon in each of the four ramekin dishes and spoon the mixture into the prepared dishes. Smooth over tops and leave to chill for 1-2 hours until set. To turn out, dip dishes in hot water and set mousse on small plates. Garnish with chives, lemon slices and tiny rolls of salmon. Serve with brown bread or toast.

SALMON AND CUCUMBER MOUSSE

(serves 6)

4"/10cm length of cucumber
1 tablespoon salt
2 x 7oz/213g cans of pink salmon (drained with bones and skin removed)
8oz/225g cottage cheese
Half pint/250ml single cream
Finely grated rind and juice of 1 lemon
Salt and freshly ground black pepper
2 teaspoons fresh chopped tarragon
Half ounce/12g sachet of gelatine
Sprig of tarragon and lemon twists to garnish
6 ramekin dishes or small moulds lightly oiled

Wash the cucumber and cut in half lengthways. Remove the seeds, grate coarsely onto a plate and sprinkle with the salt. Leave to stand for 30 minutes. Mash the salmon with a fork, rub the cottage cheese through a sieve and mix the two together with the cream. Put the grated cucumber in the sieve and rinse very thoroughly to remove all the salt. Squeeze the cucumber dry using absorbent paper and then stir into the salmon mixture. Add the lemon rind and juice and season with the salt, pepper and chopped tarragon.

Measure 3 tablespoons/45ml cold water into a cup, sprinkle the gelatine on the surface and leave to stand for 1 minute. Place the cup in a pan of gently simmering water to dissolve the gelatine, then stir into the salmon and cheese mixture. Spoon the mixture into the dishes and chill for about 1-2 hours until set. Before serving dip the dishes quickly into hot water and turn out on small dishes. Garnish with sprigs of fresh tarragon and lemon twists. Serve with salad and hot toast.

Salmon Chowder
(serves 4)

1 tablespoon/15ml vegetable or olive oil
8 spring onions (trimmed and chopped)
8oz/225g potatoes (peeled and diced)
15fl.oz/500ml chicken stock
10fl.ozs/250ml milk
Quarter teaspoon dried dill
1 tablespoon cornflour
4oz/125g frozen sweetcorn
7oz/200g can pink salmon (drained with bones and skin removed and roughly flaked)
Salt and pepper
Sprigs of dill to garnish

In a large saucepan heat the oil, add the spring onions and potatoes and cook over a moderate heat for 2-3 minutes, stirring frequently. Add the chicken stock, milk and dill, bring to the boil, lower heat, cover and leave to simmer gently for 20 minutes.

Blend the cornflour with a little water and add to the soup with the frozen sweetcorn and continue cooking for 5 minutes. Stir the salmon into the soup and heat gently for 2-3 minutes. Season and serve garnished with sprigs of dill.

SMOKIE PLATTER WITH CROUTONS
(serves 4)

3 thin slices white bread with crusts removed
Grated rind of 2 lemons
1oz/25g butter
2 tablespoons/30ml creamed horseradish
6 tablespoons/90ml single cream
Dash of Worcester sauce
6oz/175g smoked mackerel fillets
3oz/75g sliced smoked salmon
5oz/150g mixed salad leaves
Lemon wedges to serve

To make the croutons, cut the bread into small squares and toss in the lemon rind. Heat the butter in a pan and fry the bread until golden. Drain on kitchen paper.

Put the horseradish, cream, Worcester sauce and seasoning in a bowl and mix thoroughly. Pour mixture into a jug and leave to chill. Flake the mackerel and cut the salmon into strips. When ready to serve toss the fish, salad and croutons together and arrange on individual plates, garnished with lemon wedges. Serve the sauce separately.

SALMON PATÉ
(serves 4)

8oz/225g canned red or pink salmon (drained)
5oz/150g low fat curd cheese
Few drops lemon juice
Pinch ground mace or ground nutmeg
Quarter teaspoon tabasco sauce
Freshly ground sea salt and black pepper
2 tablespoons/30ml low fat fromage frais or natural yoghurt
4 small gherkins
4 ramekin dishes

Empty fish into a bowl, remove all bones and skin and with the back of a spoon work the fish into a smooth paste. In a separate bowl beat the curd cheese until it is smooth and to this add the salmon, lemon juice, seasonings and fromage frais or natural yoghurt and mix thoroughly. Divide the mixture equally between the four individual dishes, smoothing the surfaces carefully.

Slice each gherkin lengthways 4 or 5 times making sure not to cut through the narrow end. Splay the cut ends into a fan and use to decorate the tops of the pâtés in the ramekins.

TROUT
STARTERS

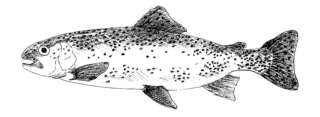

SMOKED TROUT PATÉ
(serves 4)

2 x 10oz/275g smoked trout (skinned and boned)
2oz/50g butter (softened)
2 tablespoons/30ml lemon juice
4 tablespoons/60ml single cream
Pepper
Pinch ground mace
Lemon and cucumber slices to garnish
4 ramekin dishes

Put the trout flesh in a food processor, add the butter, lemon juice, cream, pepper and mace and blend until smooth. Put the mixture in equal quantities in the ramekin dishes. Allow to chill for at least one hour before serving and garnish with the lemon and cucumber slices. Serve with fingers of toast.

TROUT MOUSSE
(serves 4-6)

4 smoked or poached trout (bones and skin removed)
6-8 stalks of celery (finely chopped)
1oz/25g gelatine
10fl.ozs/250ml white wine or wine and fish stock
1 green pepper (blanched, deseeded and diced)
1 tablespoon/15ml horseradish cream
Salt & pepper
10fl.ozs/250ml lightly whipped cream

Flake trout carefully and mix with the celery. Dissolve gelatine in half of the white wine or wine and fish stock over a low heat and then add the remaining liquid. Stir gently into the trout and celery mixture, add the pepper and horseradish cream. Fold in the cream and put into a mould. Allow to set and garnish with sliced cucumber. Serve with brown bread.

Rolled Trout in Lime and Tarragon

(serves 8)

8 small trout fillets (washed and patted dry)
1 small bunch fresh tarragon
4 bay leaves
8 black peppercorns
1 tablespoon/20g granulated sugar
1 small onion (peeled and thinly sliced)
3 limes
10fl.ozs/250ml tarragon vinegar

To serve:
1 tablespoon fresh chopped tarragon
6 tablespoons/90ml olive oil
Lettuce leaves and tarragon sprigs to garnish

Roll trout from the head to the tail, skin side out and secure with a cocktail stick. Pack close together in a deep plastic container with a few sprigs of tarragon, bay leaves, peppercorns, sugar and onion. Finely pare the rind and squeeze juice from two of the limes and add to the fish with the tarragon vinegar. Firmly cover and chill for 24 hours.

When ready to serve, arrange the rolled trout on a large serving dish or individually. Strain the marinade and measure 2 tablespoons/30ml into a small bowl. Add the chopped tarragon and olive oil and whisk until thoroughly combined. Spoon a little over each rolled trout and garnish with fine shreds of lime rind, lettuce leaves, sprigs of tarragon and slices of lime.

TROUT AND CUCUMBER MOUSSE

(serves 8)

1 cucumber (deseeded and diced)
2 tablespoons/1oz coarse salt
Half ounce/11g sachet powdered gelatine
5fl.ozs/125ml medium dry white wine
8oz/225g trout fillets (skinned)
8oz/225g full-fat soft cream cheese
2 teaspoon/10ml tarragon vinegar
1 teaspoon caster sugar
5fl.ozs/125ml double cream (lightly whipped)
Salt and pepper

Put cucumber in a colander, sprinkle with salt and leave to stand for 30 minutes. Rinse thoroughly and pat dry with absorbent paper. Sprinkle gelatine on 4 tablespoons/60ml of the wine and leave to thicken. Put the trout fillets in a small pan and pour over the remaining wine. Simmer gently for 5-8 minutes until the fish is just cooked. Allow to cool and then put fish and liquor in a blender or food processor and purée. Heat the gelatine gently over a pan of simmering water until dissolved, stirring occasionally. Beat the cream cheese, fish purée, tarragon vinegar, sugar and dissolved gelatine until thoroughly blended. Fold in the cream with the cucumber and season to taste. Spoon mixture into a wetted mould and place in refrigerator to set.

To serve, remove from mould and garnish with finely sliced lettuce or frisée and cucumber. Serve with toast.

SMOKED TROUT MOUSSE WITH A BITE

(serves 6)

2 smoked trout with flesh flaked from the bones
2 teaspoons/10ml gelatine
4 tablespoons/60ml water
5fl.ozs/125ml single cream
2 teaspoons dried horseradish
3 tablespoons/45ml lemon juice
Freshly ground black pepper
10fl.ozs/250ml double cream (whipped)
2 egg whites (whipped until stiff)
Chopped parsley or lemon slices to garnish

Put water in a small pan, sprinkle over the gelatine and heat very slowly to dissolve. Put fish in a food processor or liquidizer and whiz. Add the single cream, lemon juice horseradish and black pepper and blend again. Add the dissolved gelatine and pour into a bowl. Fold in the whipped cream and then, using a metal spoon, fold in the egg whites until thoroughly mixed. Pour mixture into a bowl, or ramekin dishes if serving individually, and leave to set. Garnish if desired with chopped parsley or slices of lemon and serve with brown bread and butter.

SMOKED TROUT PASTE

6oz/150g smoked trout flesh (with skin and bones removed)
3oz/75g softened butter
Juice of half a lemon
Salt and pepper
Pinch of mace

Mash the flesh until very fine and then work in the butter, lemon juice and seasoning. If you find any small bones, remove them. Pack the paste into small pots and cover the tops with clarified butter - melted but not hot. Can be kept refrigerated for about 2 days. Garnish as desired.

SALMON
MAIN COURSES

SALMON & VEGETABLE SALAD
(serves 4)

12oz/350g salmon or salmon trout fillets (you must have very fresh fish for this recipe)
2 carrots (peeled and finely diced)
1 large courgette (peeled and finely diced)
1 large turnip (peeled and finely diced)
Fresh coriander (chopped)
3 tablespoons/45ml tarragon or sherry vinegar
Salt and pepper
Pinch cayenne pepper
3 tablespoons/45ml olive oil
Whole coriander leaves for garnish

Skin the salmon fillet and cut fish into 1"/2.5cm pieces. Place in a bowl, add the vinegar and stir well. Leave to stand for at least 2 hours. This will allow the fish to marinate and it should appear opaque and 'cooked' by this time.

Place diced carrots in boiling water for five minutes, adding the courgette and turnip for the last minute of cooking time; then drain.

Add the coriander, oil, salt and peppers to the fish and mix in the vegetables, stirring carefully so as not to break up the fish. Chill mixture before serving and garnish with coriander leaves.

SALMON WITH FENNEL SAUCE
(serves 4)

4 x 6oz/175g salmon steaks
2 shallots (skinned and finely chopped)
1 small fennel bulb (finely chopped)
1 bay leaf
2 stalks fresh parsley (crushed)
6fl.ozs/150ml dry white wine
2 egg yolks
4oz/100g butter (softened)
Salt & pepper
Lemon juice (to taste)
Fresh fennel sprigs (to garnish)

Set oven at 180C/350F/Gas Mark 4

Place salmon steaks in a lightly greased ovenproof dish, sprinkle over the shallots, fennel, bay leaf and crushed parsley. Pour over the wine and cover tightly. Bake for 15 minutes until the fish is tender. Turn off the oven. Strain off 4fl.oz/100ml of the cooking liquor into a small pan, leaving fish and remaining liquor in dish, cover and return to oven to keep warm. Boil the strained liquor until reduced to about 1 tablespoon/15ml. Beat the egg yolks together, add the reduced liquor and work in 2oz/50g of the butter. Place bowl over a pan of hot water and whisk with a balloon whisk until the butter has melted. Gradually add the remaining butter, whisking well after each addition until you have a thick fluffy sauce. Remove pan from the heat. Take 2 teaspoons of the cooked fennel out of the dish and add to the sauce. Season to taste, adding a little lemon juice if required.

To serve, transfer salmon to a warmed serving dish and spoon the sauce over. Garnish with the fennel sprigs.

Salmon with Fresh Basil Sauce

(serves 4)

1lb/450g salmon fillets (skinned)
1 tablespoon/15ml sunflower oil
Quarter teaspoon salt
Freshly ground black pepper
1.5 tablespoons/25ml fresh lemon juice
2 shallots (thinly sliced)
1 garlic clove (finely chopped)
4oz/125g basil leaves
4 tablespoons/60ml fish stock or dry white wine
4 tablespoons/60ml double cream

Rinse fillets under cold water and pat dry. Cut fish diagonally across the grain into slices about 1"/2.5cm thick. Pour the oil into a large heavy frying pan and heat well. Add the fish pieces and cook them on one side for three minutes. Turn them over carefully and sprinkle with a little salt, a generous grinding of black pepper and lemon juice. Cook them on the second side until barely done – about three minutes more. Remove pan from the heat.

Lay fish on a warmed serving platter and cover with foil. Return the pan to a medium heat, add the shallots and garlic and cook them, stirring continuously for 30 seconds. Add the basil and the stock or wine and simmer mixture for one minute. Stir in the cream, the remaining salt and more ground pepper and continue simmering until sauce thickens slightly, about 2 minutes. Pour the sauce over the fish and serve immediately.

POACHED SALMON IN COURT BOUILLON

This recipe allows for a large fish and it is best to use a fish kettle. However if you do not have a fish kettle a large pot can be used for a piece of salmon and this should be wrapped in muslin or cheesecloth leaving a generous length at either end to use as handles.

For the court bouillon you will need:
6 pints/3 litres water
2 pints/1 litre white wine
Half pint/250ml wine vinegar
3 onions (peeled and with 3 cloves stuck in each)
3 carrots (peeled and sliced)
2 large stalks of celery (chopped) or the tops and leaves from a bunch of celery
2 bay leaves
5-6 large sprigs of parsley
1 tablespoon salt

NB. Reduce the quantities comparatively if you are only cooking a piece of fish, 1 large salmon or piece of salmon.

Bring all the ingredients except the fish to the boil and allow to simmer for an hour. Place the fish in the pot and turn up heat until it is simmering again. Cover and leave to cook allowing 8 minutes per 1lb/450g. Remove the fish carefully and if you wish to skin it, do so while it is still warm.

The court bouillon can be used to make a sauce or in aspic.

Poached salmon can be served with the following sauces – Hollandaise Sauce, Mousseline Sauce, White Sauce, Sauce Verte (see pages 107-110).

SALMON STEAKS IN WHITE WINE - 1
(serves 4)

4 x 6ozs/150g salmon steaks thickly cut
Seasoned flour
1.5oz/40g butter
5fl.ozs/125ml dry white wine

Dust steaks lightly with the seasoned flour. Melt butter in a heavy pan and when bubbling, cook steaks quickly on each side. Pour in the wine and allow to simmer, basting frequently, for about 20 minutes. Serve with plain vegetables - boiled pototoes, green vegetables or sliced cucumber.

SALMON WITH WHITE WINE - 2
(serves 4)

4 x 6oz/150g steaks
1oz/25g butter
Wine glass of dry white wine (Muscadet or dry Anjou)
Salt & pepper

Season the steaks with the salt and pepper. Put butter in a thick pan and cook the salmon slices rapidly on each side. Pour the wine over the steaks, let it bubble, reduce the heat and cook gently for about seven minutes. The sauce should be reduced by this time. Serve with plain boiled potatoes and sliced cucumber.

GRILLED SALMON STEAKS WITH SAVOURY BUTTERS
(serves 4)

4 x 6oz/150g salmon steaks
Salt and pepper
Oil or melted butter for basting

Season the steaks and brush with oil or melted butter. Leave to stand for about 15 minutes to absorb the seasoning. Place under a medium grill about 3"/7cm from the heat and cook for about 4 minutes either side. Turn steaks over carefully and baste frequently. Place on a warmed serving dish and serve with a selection of the following butters.

Lemon and Parsley Butter:
4oz/100g softened butter
2 tablespoons finely chopped parsley
Juice of half a lemon
Salt and pepper to taste

Work all the ingredients together in a bowl until thoroughly mixed. Chill before serving.

Mustard Butter:
4oz/100g softened butter
1 teaspoon/5ml Dijon mustard
Juice of half a lemon
Salt and pepper to taste
A little finely chopped parsley

Mash all the ingredients thoroughly in a bowl and chill before serving.

Brown Butter:
4oz/100g butter
Juice of half a lemon

Melt the butter in a small pan and cook until it is light brown. Add the lemon juice and serve.

Anchovy Butter:
4oz/100g Anchovy fillets (finely pounded)
4oz/100g unsalted butter (softened)

Mix both ingredients until thoroughly blended, put in a small dish and set aside in a cool place until needed.

Watercress Butter:
4oz/100g softened butter
3-4 tablespoons watercress
Half a teaspoon of lemon juice
Salt and pepper to taste

Remove the stalks from the watercress and using only the leaves, dry them and chop finely. Mash all the ingredients together until thoroughly blended and serve chilled.

BAKED SALMON STEAKS IN CREAM
(serves 4)

2 x 2"/5cm thick steaks or 4 x 1"/2.5cm thick
Salt
10fl.ozs/250ml fresh or sour cream
1 tablespoon/15ml lemon juice
1 tablespoon finely chopped dill leaves
1-2 tablespoons Dijon mustard (optional)
Finely chopped parsley

Set oven 180C/350F/Gas Mark 4

Sprinkle steaks with salt and place in a baking dish. Mix other ingredients with the exception of the parsley and pour over the steaks. Place in oven and cook for about 30 minutes. When cooked, sprinkle with parsley.

SALMON STEAKS WITH MUSHROOMS AND ONIONS

(serves 4)

4 x 1"/2.5cm steaks
Salt
A little melted butter
3fl.oz/70ml red wine
Water
Slice of onion
Slice of garlic
Sprig of parsley
4 peppercorns
2 egg yolks
4 tablespoons/60ml cream
2oz/50g butter
Salt and pepper
Squeeze of lemon juice

To garnish:
4oz/100g small white onions (skinned and cooked in boiling water until soft)
4oz/100g small mushrooms
2oz/50g butter
Finely chopped parsley

Set oven at 180C/350F/Gas Mark 4

Place steaks in a greased ovenproof dish and sprinkle with salt. Brush with melted butter and place under grill until they are golden. Add the wine and enough water to come just to the top of the steaks, then add the slice of onion, garlic, parsley and peppercorns. Cover with butter paper and bake for about 15 minutes.

While steaks are cooking prepare the garnish. Saute the onions and mushrooms in butter until the onions are lightly golden and set aside in a warm place.

When the salmon is cooked, strain off liquid and discard onion, garlic, parsley and peppercorns; keep the salmon warm. Reduce the liquid by heating to about 3fl.ozs/70ml. Put egg yolks in a bowl, beat with the cream and slowly add the liquid. Continue beating over hot water until sauce has thickened. Then beat in the butter and season with salt and pepper, stir in lemon juice.

Place mushrooms and onions around the cooked salmon and pour over the sauce. Garnish with chopped parsley.

POTATO & SALMON PIE
(serves 4-6)

12oz/300g salted salmon
2lbs/900g boiled potatoes (sliced)
20fl.oz/500ml milk
3 eggs
1 dessertspoon chopped dill or slices of lemon
White milled pepper
5oz/120g butter

Set oven at 170C/325F/Gas Mark 3.

Soak the salmon for 12 hours in a solution of equal quantities of milk and water to remove the salt. Remove fish, pat it dry and cut into equal slices. Grease a pie dish and line it with a layer of the sliced potatoes. Add a layer of the sliced salmon and then continue in layers, ending with the potatoes. Sprinkle each layer with pepper and dill or sliced lemon. Beat the eggs with the milk and pour over the layers of fish and potato. This should fill the dish. Cook for about half an hour or until golden brown and serve with melted butter sprinkled on the top.

SALMON STEAKS BAKED IN FOIL

Set oven at 180C/350F/Gas Mark 4.

Allow 1 x 6ozs/150g salmon steak about .75"/20mm thick per person.

Wrap each steak in very well buttered foil allowing plenty of foil around the edges to stop the juices leaking. Bake for about 15 minutes. If steaks are to be served cold allow them to cool before opening the foil.

SALMON KEDGEREE

1lb/450g salmon (flaked with bones and skin removed)
4 hard-boiled eggs (sliced)
6oz/150g rice (cooked)
2oz/50g butter
3-4 tablespoons/45-60ml cream
Salt and pepper
2-3 tablespoons chopped parsley
A little grated onion (but not if serving for breakfast)
1-2 tablespoons curry powder (or to taste)

Place all the ingredients in a double boiler and cook over hot water until thoroughly heated through, stirring occasionally.

SALMON FISHCAKES

8oz/225g salmon (all bones and skin removed)
12oz/300g potatoes (peeled, boiled, well drained and mashed)
Salt and pepper
1oz/25g butter
1 tablespoon/15ml single cream
2 tablespoons chopped parsley (optional)
Flour
Fat or oil for frying

Put salmon in a bowl and mash with the potatoes, adding the seasoning and butter. Mix well. If the mixture seems dry add a little cream until it will bind together without being sticky. Shape into even-sized cakes and dust with flour. Fry in heated fat or oil until golden brown, ensuring they have heated thoroughly. Serve immediately.

SALMON QUICHE

2 tablespoons minced shallots or salad onions
1¹/₂oz/40g butter
4oz/100g mushrooms (sliced)
4oz/100g flaked salmon
Salt & pepper
2 tablespoons/30ml Madiera or white vermouth
3 eggs
8oz/200ml thick cream
1 tablespoon/15ml tomato paste
A little parsley or dill (optional)
1 x 8"/20cm partially cooked pastry shell
2oz/50g Swiss cheese (grated)

Set oven at 190C/375F/Gas Mark 5.

Cook the onions gently in the butter but do not allow to brown. Add sliced mushrooms, cook for a minute or two, then add salmon, salt, pepper and Madeira or wine. Cook for a few minutes and then leave to cool slightly.

   Beat eggs with the cream, tomato paste, seasoning and herbs if liked and gradually add the salmon mixture. Put pastry shell on a baking dish and carefully pour in the filling. Sprinkle top with cheese and bake for about 25-30 minutes until puffed and golden brown.

NB. The proportions of salmon and mushrooms may be varied as you wish.

SALMON WITH ORANGE SAUCE
(serves 4)

4 salmon steaks (about 4–5ozs/100–125g each)
1 teaspoon cornflour
1 teaspoon demerara sugar
Finely grated rind and juice of 1 orange
Half teaspoon cinnamon
5fl.ozs/125ml natural yoghurt

Set oven at 190C/375F/Gas Mark 5.

Wash and pat dry the salmon steaks and place on an oiled or lightly buttered foil. Fold up to make a parcel, pinching the edges together to prevent it leaking. Place on a baking tray and cook for about 15 minutes. The flesh should appear opaque when it is cooked. Make the sauce while the fish is cooking. Put grated orange rind in a pan with the juice, sugar and cinnamon, mix in the cornflour to make a smooth paste and add the yoghurt gradually. Heat gently until mixture thickens but does not boil. Serve sauce round the salmon steaks.

SALMON IN PASTRY WITH VERMOUTH & DILL SAUCE

6 x 5-6oz/150–175g slices of fresh salmon
1lb/450g puff pastry
1 egg yolk mixed with 1 teaspoon water

For the mousse:
8oz/250g sole (skinned and chopped roughly)
1 egg
1 egg white
Half pint/250ml double cream

For the sauce:
3fl.oz/75ml Vermouth
Quarter pint/150ml fish stock
2 tablespoons/30ml thick cream
4oz/125g unsalted butter (softened)
Fresh or dried dill to taste

Prepare mousse first. Put sole with egg and egg white in a food processor and mix well. Stir in the cream.

Set oven at 230C/450F/Gas Mark 8.

Spread the mousse about quarter inch thick on top of each salmon slice. Roll out the pastry very thin and cut into six squares. Each piece of pastry should be large enough to wrap around each portion of salmon with an overlap all round of about half an inch/5cms. Place salmon portions on squares, mousse side down, wet the edges of the pastry and fold over. Seal edges well. Brush each pastry parcel with the egg wash. Place on a baking sheet, mousse side up and bake for about 10 minutes until the pastry is lightly browned and cooked.

To make the sauce put the vermouth and fish stock in a pan, heat until reduced to about half. Add the cream, mix well and gradually add the butter in small pieces, stirring all the time. Adjust consistency by adding more butter or fish stock. Add the dill and adjust to your taste.

SALMON WITH DEVIL SAUCE
(serves 4)

4 x 5-6oz/125-150g steaks
Salt & pepper
Olive oil
2oz butter
Half teaspoon Dijon mustard
Juice of half a lemon
Cayenne pepper
Chopped parsley

Mix together the butter, mustard, lemon juice, pepper and chopped parsley and refrigerate until needed.

Season steaks with the salt and pepper, brush with the olive oil and grill them gently for about seven minutes, turning once and basting with the oil. Transfer to a heated dish. Serve immediately with the mustard butter dotted on top of each steak.

SALMON ON A BED OF RICE
(serves 6)

6 x 8oz/250g slices salmon
Salt and pepper
8oz/250g cooked rice
8oz/250g button onions
4oz/125g butter
12fl.oz/340ml white wine
12fl.oz/340ml white sauce made with fish stock (see page 107)
Parsley (fried)

Season salmon with salt and pepper and poach gently in the white wine and butter. Cook the button onions in butter and keep warm. When cooked, drain salmon and arrange on a warmed serving dish on a bed of cooked rice. Reduce the poaching stock by boiling fast and add the white sauce. Garnish with the cooked onions and fried parsley. Serve immediately.

BAKED SALMON

1 Salmon
Butter
1 lemon
Dry white wine

Set oven at 180C/350F/Gas Mark 4 and allow 15 minutes per 1lb/450g.

Rinse salmon under running water and check it is completely cleaned inside. Cut off the head just behind the first set of fins, cutting at a slight angle. Cut off the tail at its narrowest point. Line a baking dish or roasting tin with foil and dot the skin and cavity of the fish with butter. Slice half a lemon and tuck into the cavity and squeeze juice from the other half over the salmon. Pour over a little white wine and fold edges of the foil tightly together, leaving salmon surrounded by a pocket of air. Bake for calculated cooking time. Check that fish is cooked as for the poached fish and leave to cool in the foil. Remove carefully when cooled and peel away the skin from both sides. Using a sharp knife scrape away the darker flesh working towards the tail and remove any fat lying along the back and cavity. Cut along the line of the flesh just above the bone to halve the fish. Ease the flesh away from the bones and lift the fillet on a broad palette knife. Set aside on your serving dish. Ease the flesh from the bones on the other side and slipping a small knife under the exposed back bone at the tail end carefully loosen from the remaining fish. Place with the other fillets and serve with garnish and sauce of your choice.

BRAISED SALMON WITH PINK SAUCE
(serves 6)

1 x 2lb2oz/1kg Fillet of salmon or 6 x 6oz/150g slices
1 tablespoon chopped shallots
Salt & pepper
10fl.oz/250ml tomato juice
10fl.oz/250ml white wine
10fl.oz/250ml single cream
8oz/250g butter
2 tablespoons/30ml Hollandaise sauce (see page 109)
2 tablespoons chopped chives
A little flour and butter (for thickening the sauce)
12 white asparagus tips

Set oven at 170C/325F/Gas Mark 3.

Generously butter a large ovenproof dish, sprinkle the shallots into the bottom and place the fillet of salmon (skin side up) or slices on top. Season with the salt and pepper, pour over the white wine and tomato juice and cover with buttered paper. Braise in the oven until cooked (this will vary depending whether you have used a whole fillet or separate slices). When cooked peel away the skin from the fish and arrange on a warmed serving dish. Put the fish stock in a pan and bring to the boil until it is reduced by half. Thicken sauce with a little flour and butter, add the cream and continue to reduce quantity. Stir the sauce briskly with the butter and hollandaise sauce, adding the chives when it is smooth and pale pink in colour. Coat the fish with the sauce and pop under the grill to slightly glaze. Garnish with the asparagus tips and serve with cooked rice.

SALMON PIE

2lb/800g salmon (cut into cubes with all bones and skin removed)
3 or 4 hard-boiled eggs (optional)
8oz/200g shrimps (optional)
1-2 tablespoons grated onion
3 tablespoons chopped parsley
Salt, pepper, paprika
1pt/500ml White Sauce (see page 107)
2oz/100ml white wine, vermouth, sherry or madeira
Creamy mashed potatoes or rich pastry

Set oven at 220C/475F/Gas Mark 7.

Place salmon, eggs and shrimps (if used), onion, parsley, salt, pepper and paprika in a casserole and mix together. Make the sauce, add the wine to it and pour over the mixture. Cover with either mashed potatoes or rich pastry (if using pastry then brush with beaten egg) and place in oven for 15 minutes, then lower heat to 180C/375F/Gas Mark 5 and cook for a further 15 minutes until nicely browned.

QUICK SALMON PIE

Set oven at 170C/325F/Gas Mark 3.

Mash cooked fish well with a fork and place a layer in a well-buttered ovenproof dish. Cover with mashed pototoes which have been well seasoned with salt and black pepper, and then a layer of finely shredded onion. Repeat the layers until the dish contains sufficient quantity for your meal, leaving about half an inch/1cm at the top. Pour over a thick layer of white sauce. Bake for about an hour.

NB. Tinned salmon can be used if liked.

SALMON STEAKS IN A CREAM SAUCE
(serves 4)

4 x 1"/2.5cm thick salmon steaks
2 tablespoons fresh chopped parsley
2 teaspoons grated lemon rind
Salt & pepper
1 bay leaf
Half pint/375ml single cream

Set oven at 190C/375F/Gas Mark 5

Grease a shallow oven proof dish and arrange the steaks in a single layer. Sprinkle with the parsley, lemon rind, salt and pepper and put the bay leaf on the top. Pour over the cream and bake for 25 minutes, basting occasionally. Serve immediately with new potatoes and peas.

GRILLED SALMON WITH BEARNAISE SAUCE

(serves 6)

6 x 8ozs/200g slices salmon
3ozs/75g butter (clarified)
6fl.oz/150ml bearnaise sauce (see page 108)
Parsley
Flour

Season salmon slices with salt and pepper, sprinkle over the flour and brush with the clarified butter. Grill gently, basting frequently with the butter. Arrange on a warmed serving dish and garnish with the parsley. Serve the sauce separately.

SALMON AND EGG MAYONNAISE SALAD

(serves 6)

1lb 8oz/600g cooked salmon with bones and skin removed
Lettuce
12oz/300g mayonnaise (see page 109)
6-8 anchovy fillets
3 hard boiled eggs
12 pitted olives
1oz/25g capers
Fresh chopped parsley (if available)

Arrange coarsely sliced lettuce in a salad bowl and season lightly. Flake the salmon and arrange on the lettuce. Cover with mayonnaise and garnish with the anchovies, olives, capers and quartered hard boiled eggs. Sprinkle over with parsley.

POTATO NESTS WITH SALMON
AND BROCCOLI
(serves 6-8)

12oz/300g fillet of salmon (skin and bones removed and cut into small pieces)
6oz/150g broccoli
10fl.ozs/250ml milk
1oz/25g butter
1oz/25g plain flour
1 teaspoon chopped fresh dill and a few sprigs
1lb 8oz/800g cooked potatoes
1 egg yolk
2 tablespoons/30ml single cream

Cut broccoli into small florets and put in pan with the chopped salmon. Pour over milk, bring to the boil and simmer for one minute. Separate the salmon and broccoli and set aside; reserve the milk. Melt butter in a pan, stir in the flour and gradually blend in the milk. Heat and continue stirring until thick and smooth, add the chopped dill and carefully fold in the salmon and broccoli.

Set oven at 200C/400F/Gas Mark 6.

Mash the potatoes with the egg yolk, cream and salt and pepper. On a well greased baking sheet or baking parchment arrange rounds of the mashed potato, keeping some back in a piping bag fitted with a large nozzle. Pipe the remaining mashed potato around the edge of the rounds leaving a "nest" in the middle. Bake for 20 minutes until just turning golden brown. Spoon in the salmon and broccoli filling into each nest and return to the oven for five minutes. Garnish with a sprig of dill and serve with fresh vegetables.

SALMON WITH HERB SAUCE
(serves 6)

6 x 6oz/150g salmon steaks
1 small onion (finely sliced)
1 carrot (finely diced)
Bouquet garni
8fl.oz/200ml dry white wine
8fl.oz/200ml water
Salt & pepper
8fl.oz/200ml soured cream
4 tablespoons fresh chopped mixed herbs

Put salmon steaks in a shallow pan with the onion, carrot and bouquet garni, pour over the wine and water, add the salt and pepper and bring slowly to the boil. Cover and allow to simmer for 15 minutes. Lift salmon steaks out carefully and place in a warmed serving dish with a lid. Keep warm. Strain the remaining liquid and reduce to about two tablespoons/30ml by boiling fast for a few minutes. Add the soured cream and warm through, mixing thoroughly. Add the herbs and spoon the sauce over the steaks. Serve with new potatoes, carrots and/or fresh green vegetables.

PLAITS OF FISH IN TOMATO SAUCE
(serves 4)

2 x 4oz/125g salmon fillets (skinned)
2 x 4oz/125g bass fillets (skinned)
Melted butter for brushing

Tomato Sauce:
2oz/50g butter
1 medium onion (finely chopped)
8oz/225g tomatoes (skinned, quartered, seeded and finely chopped)
5fl.ozs/150ml dry white wine
5fl.ozs/150ml double cream
3 teaspoons fresh chopped dill and a few sprigs
Salt & ground black pepper

Cut each fillet into 3 long thin strips of equal thickness. Taking three strips, two of one fish and one of the other, plait them carefully together, tucking the loose ends underneath. Place on a grill rack and repeat with the remaining strips until you have four plaits of fish. Brush with melted butter and cook under a medium grill for about five minutes, brushing frequently with the butter. Remove fish from grill and set aside in a warm place.

To make the sauce, melt the butter in a shallow pan, add the onion, cover and cook gently for about ten minutes until soft. Add the tomatoes, stirring them in well and continue to cook for two minutes. Add the white wine and simmer until reduced to about half the quantity. Pour in the cream and continue to simmer, stirring until the mixture thickens. Season with two teaspoons of the chopped dill, salt and pepper.

To serve, spoon the sauce onto four warmed serving plates and lay the fish on top. Garnish with the remaining chopped dill and sprigs. Serve with potatoes and green vegetables.

PARCELS OF ORIENTAL SALMON
(serves 4)

Half a carrot (peeled and sliced into fine strips)
Half a courgette (washed and cut into fine strips)
Half a yellow pepper (deseeded and cut into fine strips)
2 spring onions
1 tablespoon/15ml sesame oil
4 x 6-8oz/175/225g salmon steaks
2 tablespoons/30ml rice or white wine vinegar
2 tablespoons/30ml soy sauce
Quarter teaspoon 5-spice powder
Fresh ground black pepper
Sprigs of watercress
Four sheets greaseproof paper 10"x15"/25x38cm

Set oven at 190C/375F/Gas Mark 5.

Grease the paper sheets, place a salmon steak on each one and pour a little sesame oil over each one. Lay the vegetable strips on the fish. Mix the vinegar, soy sauce and powder and sprinkle a tablespoon/15ml over each salmon steak, season with the black pepper. Fold the paper over, twisting the edges together to make a tightly sealed parcel. Place on a baking tray and cook for 20-25 minutes when the paper should be puffed out and brown. Unwrap each parcel carefully and place the cooked fish and vegetables on warmed plates and garnish with watercress. Serve with new potatoes.

WHOLE POACHED SALMON

Use a fish kettle for this if you have one; alternatively you can use a large roasting tin. Allow 20 minutes per 1lb/450g. Set oven at 180C/350F/Gas Mark 4.

Use a sheet of foil large enough to well wrap the fish. Generously butter the foil and lay sprigs of parsley and slices of lemon on the foil. Lay the fish on this and put a few more sprigs of parsley, 3-4 lemon slices and a generous wedge of butter inside the fish. Put a few more parsley sprigs on the top of the fish and a further couple of slices of lemon. Wrap the fish into a parcel in the foil and place in a baking tin half filled with water. Cook for 15 minutes and then lower the heat to 130C/250F/Gas Mark 5. As soon as the calculated cooking time is reached unwrap to check if the fish is cooked by easing up the skin with 2 forks - if it lifts up easily the fish is cooked. Do not allow fish to overcook or it will be dry. Remove fish from the oven as soon as it is cooked.

If you are serving the fish cold, allow to cool in the foil. If serving hot unwrap the foil, remove the skin from the top side, slide the salmon carefully onto a warmed serving dish turning over at the same time and remove the skin from the underside. Cover with a fresh piece of buttered foil and keep warm in a "cool" oven until you are ready to serve it.

CHUNKY SALMON IN PUFF PASTRY
(serves 6-8)

2lb/900g fresh salmon cut into small chunks
2oz/50g butter
1 large onion (skinned and finely chopped)
8oz/225g button mushrooms (chopped)
2 hard-boiled eggs (shelled and chopped)
2 tablespoon finely chopped parsley
Salt and freshly ground black pepper
1lb 8oz/700g puff pastry
2oz/50g rice (cooked in chicken stock and thoroughly drained)
1 egg (beaten)

Melt the butter in a pan and cook the onion until it is soft and transparent (about 5 minutes). Add the mushrooms, for a further two minutes and set mixture aside. Mix the hard-boiled eggs and parsley together and season with salt and pepper. Place a piece of lightly buttered baking paper on a baking tray. Divide the pastry in half and roll out one piece to about 14x10"/35x25cm. Lay this on the baking paper and cover with the cooked rice, leaving a margin of at least 1"/2.5cm around the edge. Arrange the chunks of salmon on the rice and then the egg and parsley mixture, topping with the mushrooms and onion. Brush the pastry round the edges with the beaten egg.

Set the oven at 200C/400F/Gas Mark 6.

Roll out the other piece of pastry just slightly larger than the first one and lay over the top. Press the edges together firmly to seal and neaten the edges. Slash the pastry parcel across the top about 5-6 times and brush it all over with the beaten egg. Bake for about 35-40 minutes when it should be golden brown. Serve either hot or cold.

SALMON WITH SPINACH AND WALNUT STUFFING

(serves 6-8)

1 x 2lbs8oz/1.25kg fresh whole salmon (gutted and with head and tail removed if desired)
2lbs/900g fresh spinach (washed and coarse stalks removed)
1 small onion (peeled and chopped)
2oz/50g low fat margarine
2oz/50g walnuts (roughly chopped)
4oz/100g fresh white breadcrumbs
1 tablespoon fresh chopped parsley
1 tablespoon fresh chopped thyme
Quarter grated nutmeg
Salt and freshly ground black pepper
Juice of 2 lemons
Watercress sprigs and lemon slices to garnish

Opening the fish cavity, carefully cut along the slit made when it was gutted and cleaned. Place the fish, flesh down on a flat surface, spreading the underside out and pressing it down with the palm of the hand. Push the spine down towards the work surface. Turn the fish over and using a sharp knife gradually pull the backbone away from the fish, cutting it away with scissors at the ends. Remove the backbone completely and pull out any loose bones with a pair of tweezers. Lay the boned fish in the centre of a large square of lightly oiled foil and set aside.

Place spinach in a large saucepan, sprinkle with salt, cover and cook over a moderate heat for about 3 minutes; do not add any extra water. Turn spinach into a colander, drain well and press out excess moisture. Using a sharp knife chop the spinach finely. Fry the onion in about 1 tablespoon/15ml of the margarine until soft but not coloured. Stir the cooked onion into the spinach with the walnuts, breadcrumbs, herbs, nutmeg, salt, pepper and half the lemon juice. Mix well until all ingredients are thoroughly blended. Stuff the cavity of the trout firmly with the stuffing mixture, re-shaping the fish as you do so. Seal the foil over the top of the fish but do not wrap too tightly.

Set oven at 180C/350F/Gas Mark 4. Place wrapped fish in a roasting tin and bake in the preheated oven for 35 minutes.

Carefully unwrap fish and transfer to a large warmed serving dish, peeling away the skin from the exposed side of the fish. If possible remove as much as you can from the underside as well.

While the fish is hot, dot with remaining margarine, sprinkle the lemon juice over and serve with watercress and sliced lemon.

SALMON CUTLETS ITALIAN STYLE
(serves 6)

6 x 4oz/100g salmon cutlets
6oz/150g mushroom purée
2 egg yolks
Two parts fresh breadcrumbs to one part grated Parmesan cheese
Parsley to garnish
Few anchovies finely chopped

Thicken the mushroom purée with the egg yolks. Dip the cutlets in the purée and coat well with the breadcrumb and cheese mixture. Deep fry and arrange on a warmed serving dish. Garnish with the parsley and anchovies.

SALMON IN PASTRY WITH RED PEPPER SAUCE

(serves 6-8)

1 salmon about 4lbs/2kgs (filleted and tail left attached to one of the fillets)
4oz/100g wild rice
12fl.oz/300ml fish stock (see page 106) or water
Quarter teaspoon fennel seeds
Pinch salt
3oz/75g long-grain rice
2 lemons (juice extracted from 1 and the other thinly sliced)
Freshly ground black pepper
8 sheets of filo pastry (about 3oz/75g) - keep covered with a tea towel until
ready to use
1lb/450g asparagus (peeled, sliced diagonally into .75"/2cm lengths and boiled
for 2 minutes)
1 egg beaten with 1 teaspoon of water
1 tablespoon/15ml safflower oil

For the sauce:
1 tablespoon/15ml olive oil
1 garlic clove (crushed)
2 sweet red peppers (seeded, deribbed and coarsely chopped)
4fl.oz/100ml fish stock or unsalted chicken stock
2 teaspoons/10ml white wine vinegar
Pinch fennel seeds (crushed)
Pinch each of salt and pepper

Set oven at 180C/350F/Gas Mark 4.

Put the wild rice, stock or water, fennel seeds and salt in a small pan. Bring to the
boil and transfer to a heated ovenproof casserole. Bake in the oven for 25 minutes.
Stir in the long grain rice and return pan to the oven. Continue to bake for a
further 20-25 minutes until the liquid has been absorbed. Remove from the oven,
uncover dish and leave to cool.
    Increase oven heat to 200C/400F/Gas Mark 6.

Remove any small bones from the filleted fish with tweezers or a small sharp knife. Sprinkle some of the lemon juice over the fillets with ground black pepper. Place four of the pastry sheets on a lightly oiled baking sheet and lay the side of the fish with the tail on the downside. Spread a layer of the rice over the fillet and distribute the cooked asparagus over the top. Lay the top fillet down on the filling and arrange the remaining fish into a "fish head". Wrap the stacked sheets of filo around the salmon and tuck the corners under the fish. Brush the entire package with the safflower oil. Cut the remaining filo sheets into 10 strips (about 12x4"/30x10cm) and fold each strip lengthways down to one third. Lay the folded strips crosswise over the fish, tucking both ends underneath. Continue down the length of the parcelled fish and then snip one edge of each "ribbon" at half inch/1cm intervals. Brush gently with the beaten egg. Bake in the oven until the pastry has turned golden brown – about 25 minutes.

While the fish is cooking, make the sauce. Put the olive oil in large frying pan and place over a moderate heat. Add the garlic and cook for one minute, then add the peppers and cook until soft (about 2 minutes). Pour in the stock and vinegar, add the fennel seeds and seasoning. When the mixture reaches simmering point, remove from the heat. Puree the mixture in a blender or food processor and when ready to serve reheat.

Transfer the cooked fish to a warmed serving dish and garnish with the lemon slices. Allow to cool for 5 minutes before slicing and serve with the sauce.

CRISPY SALMON CUTLETS
(serves 6)

1lb/450g fresh uncooked salmon
6oz/150g white bread (soaked in milk and then squeezed out)
7oz/175g butter
Salt & pepper
1 egg (beaten)
Fresh breadcrumbs
A little flour

Chop the salmon with the soaked bread and 3oz/75g of the butter and mix until a smooth firm paste is formed. Season with salt and pepper. On a floured board shape the salmon mixture into six or twelve cutlets, brush with the beaten egg and dust with breadcrumbs. Cook in clarified butter turning them over very carefully. Arrange on a dish and serve immediately.

SALMON AND DILL TART

(serves 6-8)

4oz/125g butter (hard from the fridge and cut into small pieces)
6oz/175g flour
2 teaspoon icing sugar
1 teaspoon salt
Freshly ground black pepper

For the filling:
1lb/450g fresh salmon (cut into 1"/2.5cm cubes)
2 eggs
2 egg yolks
20fl.oz/500ml fresh single cream or milk and cream mixed
Salt & freshly ground black pepper
A few sprigs of dill

Put all the pastry ingredients in a food processor and whiz until mixture resembles fine breadcrumbs. If mixing by hand, cut up the butter with a sharp knife and rub it in with your fingers. Pat the mixture firmly around the sides and bottom of a lightly greased flan dish about 8"/20cm in diameter. Put the flan case in the fridge to chill for about 30 minutes.

Set oven at 180C/350F/Gas Mark 4 and bake for 30 minutes or until evenly cooked and golden brown.

Arrange the salmon evenly over the cooked pastry, beat the eggs, yolks, cream, salt and pepper together and pour over the salmon. Tear the dill into small pieces and scatter over the surface. Reduce oven to 170C/325F/Gas Mark 3 and return flan to the oven for 30 minutes or until the filling is just set when touched.

Can be served hot or cold.

WHOLE SALMON IN PUFF PASTRY
(serves 6-8)

1 salmon weighing about 9lb/4kgs (skinned and filleted)
1 cucumber
2 onions (peeled and finely chopped)
8fl.oz/225ml dry white wine
1lb8oz/700g puff pastry
Large bunch of parsley (finely chopped)
1 egg (beaten)

Peel the cucumber, halve it and scoop out the seeds. Dice the flesh, put in a colander and sprinkle with salt. Leave for at least 30 minutes and then drain and rinse the cucumber. Pat it dry with absorbent kitchen paper. Put the onion in a saucepan with the wine and simmer over a moderate heat for about 30 minutes when the wine will have almost disappeared. Mix the cooked onions with the parsley and cucumber.

Set oven at 200C/400F/Gas Mark 6.

Roll out the pastry, divide in half and place one sheet on a lightly buttered baking tray. Spread the onion and cucumber mixture on this pastry sheet and lay the salmon on top, tucking the tail end under so you have about the same thickness of salmon at both ends. Brush the edges of the pastry with beaten egg and lay the other sheet of pastry over the top. Crimp the edges together so they are well sealed and you have a neat oblong pastry parcel. Brush the surface with the beaten egg and cut 3 diagonal slashes across the top. Bake for about 30-35 minutes until golden brown.

Serve hot cut into slices with a sauce of your choice.

NB. This dish can be prepared a few hours before needed kept in a refrigerator. Remove it from the refrigerator about an hour before cooking.

WATERCRESS AND SALMON FILO PIE

(serves 6-8)

4oz/125g watercress with stalks removed
6 eggs
3fl.oz/75ml single cream
Salt and ground black pepper
Oil for greasing
14oz/400g packet of filo pastry (defrosted)
2 x 15oz/425g cans of pink salmon (drained with skin and bones removed)
Grated rind of 1 lemon
Juice of half a lemon
2 teaspoon fennel seeds
1 non-stick tin 11"x7"/28x18cm

Set oven at 190C/375F/Gas Mark 5.

Blanch the watercress by placing it in a sieve and pouring boiling water over it.
Drain well. Put the watercress, eggs, cream, milk and seasoning in a food processor
or blender and blend for one minute. Pour mixture into a pan and heat gently,
stirring well until it begins to scramble. Remove from the heat and set aside to cool.
Brush the tin with the oil. In a bowl mix the salmon with the lemon rind and juice.
   Gently unroll the filo pastry and separate out 14 sheets. Rewrap the rest in cling
film. Brushing the pastry sheets with oil as you work, put two sheets on the pastry in
the base of the tin with the edges overlapping the sides. Cut 12 sheets to the size of
the base and continuing to grease each sheet, lay 5 sheets in the base. Pour in half
the cooked mixture and top with the salmon mixture sprinkled over with the fennel
seeds. Spoon over the remaining watercress mixture and level top. Greasing five more
sheets of the filo pastry lay these on the mixture and fold the overlapping edges over
the top. Grease again and top with the remaining sheets. Bake for 35 - 40 minutes
until golden brown. Serve cold with salad and new potatoes.

SALMON PUFF PASTRY PIE
(serves 6)

1lb/450g cooked salmon (skin and bones removed and flesh flaked)
4 egg whites
Half teaspoon of salt
10fl.oz/250ml double cream
8oz/225g puff pastry
1 egg (beaten)

Whisk the egg whites so they are broken but not frothy. Put the salmon with the salt in a food processor or liquidizer and whiz, add the cream and whiz again until you have a smooth purée. Add the egg whites and whiz again. Lightly grease a pie dish, put the mixture in the dish and put in the fridge to chill for about an hour.

Set the oven at 200C/400F/Gas Mark 6.

Roll out the pastry, dampen the edges of the pie dish and put on pastry top, crimping the edges to seal. Brush top with beaten egg and cut 2 or 3 slashes across the top. Bake for 25-30 minutes until the pastry is puffed and golden brown. Serve immediately with Hollandaise Sauce (see page 109).

TROUT
MAIN COURSES

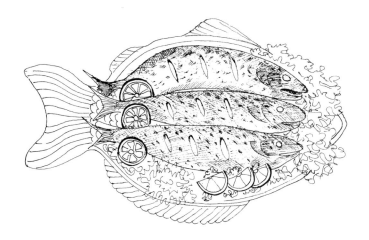

TROUT WITH MUSHROOMS AND ONIONS

(serves 4)

4 x 10oz/275 gutted trout (with heads and tails on)
Salt & freshly ground black pepper
Flour for coating
1 tablespoon/15ml oil
3oz/75g butter
2 spring onions (finely sliced)
12oz/350g mushrooms (sliced)
1 tablespoon chopped parsley
Juice of half a lemon
1oz/25g dry white breadcrumbs
Lemon quarters and sprigs of parsley to garnish

Wash trout and pat dry with absorbent paper. Season inside with salt and pepper and coat lightly with flour. Put oil and 1oz/25g of butter in a large frying pan and sauté the trout gently for 6-8 minutes on each side, until lightly browned. In another pan, melt 1.5oz/40g butter and sauté the spring onions and mushrooms until soft. Add salt, parsley and lemon juice and toss lightly.

Place trout on warmed serving dish and arrange cooked onions and mushrooms around them. Keep in a warm place while you quickly sauté the breadcrumbs until they are crisp in the frying pan you have used for the fish, adding more butter if needed. Sprinkle over the fish and garnish with lemon quarters and parsley. Serve immediately.

TROUT IN ASPIC
(serves 4)

3 pints/1.5 litres water
2 tablespoons/30ml vinegar
Pinch salt and 6 black peppercorns
2 bay leaves
2 parsley stalks
1 small onion (skinned and diced)
10fl.ozs/250ml dry white wine
4 rainbow trout each about the same size (gutted and well washed)
2 egg whites
2 levels tablespoons/1oz powdered gelatine
Lemon slices, capers and sprigs of fresh dill for garnish

Put the water, vinegar, salt, peppercorns, bay leaves, parsley stalks, onion and wine in a large saucepan or fish kettle, bring to the boil and allow to simmer for about half an hour. Allow to cool slightly and add the fish. Cover, bring back to simmering point and cook gently for 5 minutes. Leave fish to cool in the liquid, uncovered, until it is lukewarm. Carefully remove the fish, drain and remove the skin both sides while it is still warm. Strain the liquid and set aside.

Lift the fillets carefully from both sides of the trout so as not to break them up, ensuring they are free of skin and bones, and placing on one large serving dish or individual plates.

Pour the liquid from the cooked fish into a large saucepan, add the egg whites and heat mixture, whisking constantly with a balloon whisk. Bring mixture to the boil when the egg whites should form a thick frothy crust on top. Stop whisking and allow the liquid and egg whites to boil up the side of the pan, remove from heat and leave to subside. Repeat this process two more times and then leave mixture to settle.

Line a colander with several thicknesses of paper towel or an old clean tea towel, place over a bowl and pour the fish stock and egg white into the colander. Leave to drain slowly and do not allow the egg white to fall into the drained liquid. When all the liquid has drained through, take out about 10fl.ozs/250ml, put in a small pan and dissolve the gelatine, heat gently to ensure it has dissolved completely. Add the gelatine mixture to the stock and place the bowl in ice water to help thicken the mixture. Decorate the trout and base of the serving dishes with lemon slices, capers and fresh dill and when the aspic has become slightly thickened spoon carefully over the decoration to set it. Place in a refrigerator to set. When this is set, reheat the aspic very gently in a pan of hot water and stir carefully so as not to make any bubbles. Chill again and then spoon over the trout to completely cover in a layer of aspic. Return dish or dishes to the refrigerator and serve when cold and completely set.

TROUT IN TANGY SAUCE
(serves 4)

4 x 8oz/225g trout (washing and patted dry)
2fl.oz/50ml water
1 tablespoon/15ml lemon juice
Salt & ground black pepper

For the sauce:
10fl.ozs/250ml mayonnaise (see page 109)
1fl.oz/25ml tomato juice
Dash of tabasco
Salt & pepper
2oz/50g prawns

To garnish:
Half a sliced cucumber and watercress

Poach the trout for 15-20 minutes in the water, lemon juice and seasonings, and leave to cool in the liquid. Lift out and carefully remove the skin and bone. Set aside on a serving dish. Mix the tomato juice with the mayonnaise, tabasco and seasoning and add the prawns. Spoon mixture over the fish and garnish with the sliced cucumber and watercress. Serve immediately.

ITALIAN STYLE MARINATED TROUT
(serves 4)

4 x 8oz/225g whole trout (cleaned with head and tails left on)
2 tablespoon/30ml olive oil
1oz/25g flour
1 small bulb of fennel (trimmed and finely sliced)
1 onion (skinned and finely sliced)
10fl.ozs/250ml dry white Italian wine
Finely grated rind and juice of 1 orange
Salt and freshly ground black pepper
Orange slices and chopped fennel tops to garnish

Heat the olive oil in a large heavy based frying pan, dip the trout in the flour and fry gently for about 4 minutes on each side. Transfer the fish to a shallow dish. Using a sharp knife, score the skin diagonally but do not cut too deeply into the flesh. Set aside. To make the marinade, put the fennel and onion in the frying pan and cook for 5 minutes, add the wine, orange rind and juice and season to taste. Bring to the boil and boil rapidly for 1 minute, add a few chopped fennel tops and pour over the fish immdiately. Allow to cool completely and marinate for at least 8 hours but no more than 3 days.

When ready to serve, allow fish to gain room temperature and garnish with orange slices and remaining fennel tops.

RAINBOW TROUTE EN CROUTE
(serves 4)

4 x 8-10oz/225-275g rainbow trout (cleaned)
1lb/450g puff pastry
1 egg (beaten)
Small bunch watercress
1 lemon

Stuffing:
8oz/225g potatoes (mashed)
Rind and juice of 1 lemon
1 dessertspoon chopped chives
1 dessertspoon chopped tarragon
1 tablespoon chopped parsley
1 teaspoon powdered mace
Salt & pepper

Roll the pastry out thinly and cut into four rectangles (large enough to allow one trout to be parcelled into each one). Blend all the stuffing ingredients and stuff each trout with the same amount. Place each trout in the centre of each pastry rectangle and season with salt and pepper and a squeeze of lemon juice. Dampen the edges of the pastry and fold up over the fish, neatly sealing the edges.

Set the oven at 200C/400F/Gas Mark 6. Brush fish parcels with beaten egg and lay on a lightly oiled baking sheet. Bake for 20 minutes and then reduce heat to 180C/350F/Gas Mark 4 and cook for a further 25 minutes. If the pastry starts to brown too fast cover with a sheet of baking paper or foil.

When ready to serve garnish with watecress and lemon wedges.

TROUT WITH HERB SAUCE
(serves 4)

2lb/900g trout (cleaned and patted dry)
3 tablespoons/45ml lemon juice
2oz/50g butter
Salt & pepper
1 bunch watercress (trimmed and roughly chopped)
4oz/100g fresh spinach leaves (roughly chopped)
3 tablespoons chopped fresh parsley
2 tablespoons chopped fresh chervil
1 tablespoon chopped fresh dill
5fl.ozs/150ml mayonnaise (see page 109)
Fresh herbs and whole unpeeled cooked prawns to garnish

Set oven at 180C/350F/Gas Mark 4.

Place fish in the centre of a piece of foil, spoon over 2 tablespoons/30ml of lemon juice and dot with 1oz/25g of the butter. Season to taste. Wrap fish in the foil, sealing firmly, and check weight. Allowing 10 minutes per 1lb/450g calculate the baking time and cook accordingly. When cooking time is reached, take fish out of the foil, reserving the cooking liquor in a saucepan, and while still warm remove the skin carefully. Arrange the fish on a serving dish and leave to cool.

Add the remaining 1oz/25g butter to the cooking liquor and heat gently. Add the watercress, spinach, parsley, chervil and dill and cook for 2-3 minutes until softened. Pour the sauce into a food processor and blend until smooth. Transfer to a bowl and add the remaining lemon juice and season to taste. Leave mixture to cool and then fold in the mayonnaise. Put in a small serving dish and refrigerate until ready to use.

When the fish is cold, garnish with a few fresh herbs and whole prawns and serve with the herb sauce.

TROUT WITH CUCUMBER SAUCE

(serves 4)

4 x 10oz/275g trout (cleaned and patted dry)
Salt & pepper
10fl.ozs/250ml fish or vegetable stock
Half small cucumber
10fl.oz/250ml fresh soured cream
1 teaspoon/5ml tarragon vinegar
1 teaspoon fresh chopped tarragon
Fresh tarragon to garnish

Set oven at 180C/350F/Gas Mark 4.

Arrange trout in a lightly oiled ovenproof dish in a single layer, season to taste and pour over the stock. Cover and bake for about 25 minutes or until the trout are tender. Carefully lift fish out of the cooking liquor and remove the skin, leaving the heads and tails intact. Set aside to cool.

To make the sauce, coarsely grate the cucumber and then add the cream, vinegar and tarragon and season to taste. Mix thoroughly. Coat the trout with some of the sauce, leaving the heads and tails exposed. Garnish with tarragon. Serve the remaining sauce separately in a bowl. Serve immediately with potatoes and green vegetables.

STUFFED TROUT WITH A WINE SAUCE
(serves 4)

4oz/100g fresh wholemeal breadcrumbs
1 tablespoon chopped fresh herbs - parsley/thyme/rosemary*
Finely grated rind and juice of half a lemon
Pinch grated nutmeg
Salt & pepper
1 egg (beaten)
4 x 10oz/275g trout (cleaned and patted dry)
1oz/25g butter
1oz/25g flour
5fl.ozs/125ml dry white wine
5fl.ozs/125ml vegetable stock
4 tablespoons/60ml fresh double cream
*alternatively you can use marjoram, dill, tarragon or chervil.

Set oven at 180C/350F/Gas Mark 4.

Put breadcrumbs, herbs, grated lemon rind and juice and nutmeg in a bowl. Mix well and season to taste. Add the egg and blend thoroughly. Fill the cavities of the trout with the stuffing and wrap in lightly oiled foil. Place on a baking sheet and bake for 30-35 minutes until tender.

While fish is cooking, put the butter, flour, wine and stock in a saucepan and heat, whisking continuously with a balloon whisk. The sauce will gradually thicken and become smooth and allow it to lightly simmer for 1-2 minutes. Stir in the cream and season to taste.

Remove the trout carefully from their foil parcels and place on a warmed serving dish. Pour a little sauce over the cooked fish and serve immediately. Put remainng sauce in a warmed bowl or jug and serve separately.

BACON WRAPPED TROUT
(serves 4)

4 x 10oz/275g trout (cleaned and patted dry)
Salt & pepper
8 think streaky bacon rashers (with rind removed)
Chopped fresh parsley to garnish

Set oven at 200C/400F/Gas Mark 6.

Season the cavity of each fish with salt and pepper. Wind 2 bacon rashers round each fish and arrange in a shallow ovenproof dish, tucking the loose ends underneath the fish. Bake for 15-20 minutes until tender and serve immediately garnished with the chopped parsley.

SAUTÉED TROUT

Allow one trout, cleaned and patted dry, per person. Dust lightly in seasoned flour. Melt a generous portion of butter in a large pan and fry fish until cooked ensuring the skin does not burn. Serve immediately with a little butter from the pan, lemon juice and chopped parsley.

TROUT FRIED IN OATMEAL

Allow one trout about 10oz/275g with head and fins cut off, cleaned and patted dry for each person. Coat with seasoned oatmeal and fry in a mixture of butter and oil until it is brown on both sides; this will take about 4 minutes either side. The oatmeal gives a crunchy texture to the skin of the fish.

Remove from pan carefully with a fish slice and serve immediately.

BAKED TROUT WITH CREAM AND YOGHURT

Allow 2 small trout per person. Clean trout and wipe but do not wash. Fry fish quickly in a little butter until golden brown. Transfer to an ovenproof casserole.

Set oven at 170C/325F/Gas Mark 3.

For six small trout, mix 1 small carton of natural yoghurt with an equal amount of thick cream and a little salt and pepper. Pour mixture over the fish and bake for about 20 minutes. Serve immediately.

NORWEGIAN TROUT

Allow 2 small trout per person. Clean trout and wipe but do not wash. Fry fish quickly in a little butter until browned. Pour in a little thick fresh cream, season with salt and pepper and leave to simmer until fish is cooked and the sauce is thick and golden. Serve immediately.

TROUT WITH CREAM AND CHIVES
(serves 4)

4 x 8oz/225g trout (washed and patted dry)
Seasoned flour
1oz/25g melted butter
3 tablespoons/45ml double cream
Snipped chives

Set oven at 220C/425F/Gas Mark 7.

Dust trout with the flour, lay on a well oiled baking sheet and brush fish generously with the melted butter. Bake in the oven for about 8-10 minutes or until the skin is crisp, basting a couple of times. While fish is cooking pour cream into a small saucepan and heat until it thickens slightly and add a tablespoon of the snipped chives. Put the fish on warmed serving dishes and pour over the cream and chives. Serve immediately.

POACHED TROUT

This is an excellent way of cooking trout in court bouillon, particularly if you wish to serve them cold.

The ingredients for the court bouillon are as follows:
2 pints/1 litre water
15fl.oz/375ml white wine
3fl.oz/75ml wine vinegar
1 onion (peeled and with a few cloves stuck in it)
1 carrot (sliced)
1 stalk celery (sliced)
1 bayleaf
1 spring thyme
2 sprigs parsley
Salt & pepper

Mix all the ingredients in a large saucepan, bring to the boil and allow to simmer gently for about half an hour. Poach the trout gently in the court bouillon for about 4-6 minutes. If you are able to use a shallow pan for this they will be easier to remove. Serve with the sauce of your choice.

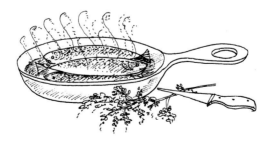

PARCEL BAKED TROUT

(serves 4)

4 fresh rainbow trout (cleaned and gutted)
8 rashers unsmoked bacon
2 teaspoons/10ml lemon juice
1 teaspoon dried marjoram
4 cobs of sweetcorn
2oz/50g butter (softened)
4 bay leaves (crushed)
1 tablespoon parsley (finely chopped)
1 lemon (for garnish)
Salt & pepper

Set oven at 220C/450F/Gas Mark 7

Remove the cobs of corn from the husks and wipe inside the husks. Mix the softened butter, bay leaves, lemon juice and seasoning thoroughly and divide into four portions. Place one portion inside each trout, sprinkle over the marjoram and wrap each fish in two rashers of bacon. Place inside the corn husk and tie securely. Bake for about 8-10 minutes, turning the parcels over once during this time. Check the fish is cooked by flaking the fish with a fork. Serve immediately and garnish with lemon wedges.

The corn cobs can be boiled separately and served with a generous knob of butter with the trout.

NB. This recipe can be cooked over a barbeque by placing the parcels over the glowing embers, turning and testing as above.

TROUT IN A STREAM
(serves 6)

6 x 8oz/225g trout (gutted and cleaned)
15fl.oz/375ml water
1 tablespoon/15ml white wine vinegar
1 onion (peeled and thinly sliced)
1 bay leaf
1 carrot (sliced)
5fl.oz/125ml dry white wine
6 peppercorns
Pinch of salt
2 sprigs each of parsley and thyme
A few fronds of fennel

Put the water, vinegar, wine, herbs, vegetables and seasoning in a pan, cover and bring to the boil. Reduce heat and allow to simmer for 30 minutes. Remove from heat and allow to cool. Put the trout in a pan in which they fit closely and strain the cooled stock over them. Bring slowly to the boil, reduce the heat and allow to simmer for about 10 minutes. Test if the fish are cooked by gently flaking the flesh with a fork. When cooked, remove carefully from the pan on to a large plate or board. When it is cool enough to handle remove the skin, heads and bones and place fillets on a clean serving dish, at least 1"/2.5cm deep. Bring the stock back to the boil and simmer briskly until the amount is reduced to about half. Lay a few fennel fronds by the fillets and strain the reduced liquid over them. Leave to set overnight in a refrigerator. The jelly will set clear and the fish with the fennel give the appearance of a clear stream.

Trout with Vermouth and Herbs
(serves 4)

4 x 8oz/225g trout (remove fins, rinse and pat dry)
2 tablespoons/30ml olive oil
Sea salt
Freshly ground black pepper
4 tablespoons/60ml dry vermouth
4 sprigs fresh herbs (dill, fennel, chives or parsley)
1 lemon

Set oven at 230C/450F/Gas Mark 8.

Season cavity of trout with salt and pepper and put in the herbs. Cut four pieces of foil large enough to take a trout each and allowing an extra 3"/7cm. Lightly grease the foil and lay the trout in the centre. Bring up the sides of the foil to make a "boat" and then brush the fish with the olive oil. Season, spoon the vermouth over each one in equal amounts and lay a slice of lemon on the top. Draw the foil edges together, fold over and pinch the edges together, making a sealed parcel. Place parcels on a baking tray and cook for about 8-10 minutes. Check fish is cooked by opening one of the parcels. When cooked serve immediately, either in the foil parcels or put fish on warmed plates and pour the cooking liquor over them.

TROUT WITH ALMONDS
(serves 4)

4 x 8oz/225g trout (washed and patted dry)
2oz/50g almonds
2oz/50g butter
Salt & ground black pepper
Lemon juice
A little watercress

Poach fish in a court bouillon as on page 115 When fish is cooked, carefully remove the skin, arrange on a heated serving dish, cover and keep warm. Blanch and shred the almonds. Heat the butter in a small pan, add the almonds and cook slowly until they are toasted a pale golden brown. Add the lemon juice, salt and black pepper to taste and pour over the fish. Garnish with watercress and serve immediately.

GRILLED TROUT WITH TARRAGON

1 trout per person (cleaned and patted dry)
Butter
Fresh tarragon

Make several diagonal cuts in the flesh of the fish on both sides and put a few tarragon leaves and a generous knob of butter in each cavity. Leave fish aside for an hour or so to absorb the flavour of the herb. Melt a little butter, brush over the trout and put under a hot grill for about 4 minutes each side. Serve immediately with melted butter and lemon juice with a green salad.

TROUT WITH CUCUMBER
AND SPINACH SAUCE
(serves 4)

4 x 8oz/225g trout fillets
Half a glass of white wine
1fl.oz/25ml water
1 tablespoon/15ml lemon juice
1 small cucumber (diced)
2oz/50g spinach
2 sprigs of tarragon and chervil
Half ounce/15g butter
Half ounce/15g flour
10fl.ozs/250ml hot water
2 egg yolks
2oz/50g butter
2 shallots (finely chopped)

Poach the fillets in the wine, water and lemon juice with a few sprigs of tarragon and chervil. When cooked arrange on a heated serving dish, cover and keep warm.

Blanch the cucumber and boil the spinach for 5 minutes with sprigs of tarragon and chervil. Drain spinach, put in a blender or food processor and whiz. Set aside. Melt the butter in a saucepan and blend in the flour. Add the hot water, salt and pepper and the egg yolks. Stir briskly with a balloon whisk until just under boiling and gradually add 2oz/50g butter. Add the spinach purée, blending thoroughly. Put the liquor from the fish in a saucepan, add the shallots and cook fast until it has thickened slightly. Strain this into the green sauce, adding a squeeze of lemon juice and seasoning if desired. Add the cucumber and mix thoroughly. Spoon the spinach and cucumber sauce over the fish and serve immediately.

TROUT WITH BACON STUFFING
(serves 4)

4 x 8oz/225g trout (washed and patted dry)
2oz/50g butter
4 streaky bacon rashers (finely chopped)
1 small onion (peeled and finely chopped)
4oz/100g mushrooms (finely chopped)
2oz/50g fresh brown breadcrumbs
2 tablespoon fresh chopped parsley
Grated rind of 1 lemon
Salt & pepper
1 egg

Set oven at 190C/375F/Gas Mark 5.

Melt the butter in a pan, add the bacon, onion and mushrooms and cook over a low heat until soft and golden. Remove from heat and thoroughly mix in the breadcrumbs, parsley, lemon rind, salt, pepper and egg. Stuff the cavity of the fish with the mixture and secure with cocktail sticks. Put fish in a well greased oven-proof dish in a single layer and bake for 20-25 minutes. Serve immediately with boiled or sautéed potatoes and vegetables.

TROUT WITH SAGE AND MUSHROOMS
(serves 4)

4 x 8oz/225g trout (washed, patted dry and heads removed if desired)
2oz/50g butter
2oz/50g dry breadcrumbs
1 small onion (peeled and finely chopped)
2 teaspoons finely chopped fresh sage
Salt & pepper
8oz/225g button mushrooms (sliced)
5fl.oz/125ml single cream

Set oven at 180C/350F/Gas Mark 4.

Place fish in a well greased ovenproof dish and cover with buttered baking paper. Bake for 20 minutes. While fish is cooking, melt the butter in a pan, add the breadcrumbs, onion and sage and cook over a low heat until the breadcrumbs are golden brown. Season with salt and pepper. Put the mushrooms and cream in a separate pan, cover and simmer for 3 minutes. Pour the mushrooms and cream over the cooked fish with the breadcrumb mixture sprinkled on the top. Return to the oven and bake for a further five minutes. Serve immediately with potatoes and vegetables.

CRISPY TROUT
(serves 4)

4 x 8-10oz/225-250g trout (washed and patted dry)
2 medium onions (peeled and chopped)
1 tablespoon/15ml cooking oil
1 garlic clove (crushed)
Salt & pepper
1oz/25g fresh breadcrumbs
2oz/50g melted butter
2 streaky bacon rashers
1 tablespoon fresh chopped parsley

Set oven at 180C/350F/Gas Mark 4.

Fry the onions in the oil until soft and golden, stir in the garlic and season well. Put trout in a well greased ovenproof dish and cover with the onion mixture. Mix the breadcrumbs with the melted butter, add salt and pepper and sprinkle over the onion mixture. Bake for 25 minutes. While the trout are cooking grill the bacon until crisp and crumble into small pieces. Sprinkle the bacon and chopped parsley on the fish and serve immediately with boiled potatoes and vegetables.

BAKED TROUT WITH HERBS
(serves 6)

6 x 8oz/225g trout (washed and patted dry)
6oz/150g fresh breadcrumbs
3oz/75g onion (peeled and chopped)
1 teaspoon chopped parsley
Pinch each of sweet marjoram and sage
Salt & pepper
6 large field mushrooms
6oz/150g cucumber
1 egg and 1 egg yolk (beaten together)
2oz/50g butter
2 lemons
Flour

Set oven at 180C/350F/Gas Mark 4.

Mix the breadcrumbs with the onion and herbs, add the beaten egg and season with salt and pepper. Stuff the cavity of the trout, coat with flour and arrange on a well buttered oven proof dish. Bake for 25-30 minutes, checking they are cooked through and serve garnished with grilled mushrooms and cucumber, grooved but not peeled and thinly sliced, and quarters of lemon. Serve immediately.

FRIED TROUT
(serves 6)

12 very small trout (about 4oz/100g each)
2 eggs (beaten)
Chopped parsley (fried)
Fresh breadcrumbs
2 lemons
Flour
10fl.oz/250ml mayonnaise or sauce tartare (see pages 109 and 111)

Clean and dry the trout. Season with salt and pepper, dip in flour, then egg and coat with breadcrumbs. Fry in hot deep oil and drain well. Arrange on a warmed serving dish and serve immediately with fried parsley and quarters of lemon.

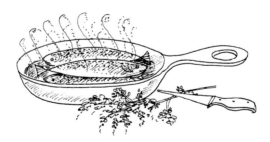

TROUT WITH GRAPES

(serves 6)

6 x 8oz/225g trout (washed and patted dry)
Salt & pepper
10fl.oz/250ml white wine
3oz/75g butter
2oz/50g beurre manié (see page 106)
8oz/225g white seedless grapes (peeled)
1 teaspoon finely chopped mixed herbs of your choice

Season the trout with salt and pepper and poach in the wine and 2oz/50g butter. While fish are poaching, heat the grapes in the remaining butter. Remove fish from pan, arrange on a heated serving dish and garnish with the grapes. Return the pan with the poaching stock to the heat, bring to the boil and keep at a simmering boil until it is reduced by about a quarter. Thicken it slightly with the beurre manie, season to taste and when the sauce is smooth, pour over the fish. Sprinkle with the chopped herbs and serve immediately.

TROUT WITH CAPERS AND TOMATOES
(serves 6)

6 x 8oz/225g trout (cleaned and patted dry)
8oz/225g capers
4oz/100g tomatoes (peeled, de-seeded and chopped)
Freshly ground black pepper
3fl.oz/75ml white wine
Juice of 1 lemon
1oz/25g butter
Butter
6 sheets baking paper lightly oiled (large enough to roll each trout in)

Set oven at 180C/350F/Gas Mark 4.

Remove the head and bones from the trout and open the fish flat, skin side down. Mix the capers with the tomatoes and season with salt and pepper. Distribute the mixture over the trout, roll and tie up each fish in the oiled paper. Grease a shallow ovenproof dish and lay the trout parcels in a single layer. Sprinkle over the wine, add the bayleaf, cover and poach in the oven for about 10-15 minutes. When cooked remove the fish carefully out of their parcels and arrange on a serving dish. Put the cooking liquor in a small saucepan, heat to a simmering boil and allow to reduce slightly. Add the lemon juice and leave to cool. When cold pour over the fish.

NB. This dish can also be served hot with rice.

Barbequed Trout
(serves 4)

4 x 8oz/225g trout (cleaned, patted dry and fins removed)
1oz/25g fresh chopped parsley
2 cloves garlic (crushed)
1 egg (beaten)
4oz/125g fresh breadcrumbs
Salt & pepper
4oz/125g melted butter
1 lemon (sliced)
1 lime (sliced)
Sprigs of fresh dill to garnish

Mix together the parsley, garlic, egg, breadcrumbs and seasoning. Divide the mixture equally and stuff the cavity of each trout. Brush the fish with the melted butter and lay lemon and lime slices on the top. Put in a fish grill if you have one and grill or barbeque for 5-6 minutes each side, turning over carefully. Serve immediately garnished with the dill. Can be served with salad, baked potato or corn on the cob.

Alternatively, the fish can be wrapped in foil and baked in the embers of the barbeque. Leave to cook for about 5-6 minutes.

Rainbow Trout with Almonds and Cream

(serves 6)

6 rainbow trout (cleaned and dried but with heads and tails left on)
3oz/75g flaked almonds
10fl oz/250ml double cream
Salt and freshly ground black pepper
2oz/50g butter
1 tablespoon/15ml cooking oil
Chopped chives to garnish (if desired)

Over a moderate heat, brown the almonds, shaking the pan to prevent them burning. When fairly evenly toasted, add the cream and simmer for 3-5 minutes. Season with salt and pepper. Melt the butter and oil in a pan until bubbling and fry the trout for 2 minutes on either side. Remove the heads and tails and lift off the skin - this should come away easily as the fish cooks. Place on a heated serving dish and pour over the cream and almond sauce. Serve immediately.

TROUT STUFFED WITH CHOPPED MUSHROOMS
(serves 4)

4 fresh trout (gutted, cleaned and patted dry)
8oz/225g mushrooms finely chopped
1 medium size onion (peeled and finely chopped)
2oz/50g butter
2 tablespoons chopped parsley
Salt & freshly ground black pepper
2 lemons
A few sprigs of parsley to garnish

Set oven at 180C/350F/Gas Mark 4.

Melt butter in a frying pan, add the onion and cook until soft and transparent (about 3 minutes). Add the mushrooms and cook for a further two minutes. Stir in the chopped parsley and seasoning. Pour mixture through a sieve and keep the liquor to use later. Divide the mixture into 4 equal quantities and stuff each trout. Lay fish on four separate pieces of foil lined with greased kitchen paper. Add the lemon juice to the liquid and spoon over each fish, add seasoning to taste. Pull the foil securely around each fish and place parcels in a single layer in a baking tin. Cook for 25-30 minutes. Unwrap parcels and serve fish on a warmed serving dish garnished with lemon wedges and parsley sprigs.

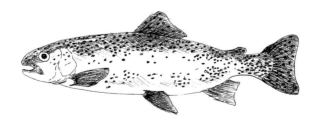

COLD RAINBOW TROUT
WITH CUCUMBER SAUCE
(serves 4)

1 rainbow trout per person (gutted, washed and dried with tails removed)
1 lemon
1 bay leaf
Sprig each of parsley and thyme
A few black peppercorns
Slice of onion and carrot

For the sauce:
Half a small cucumber
Salt and pepper
5fl.oz/300ml natural yoghurt

Using a pan large enough to hold the trout in a single layer, put in a wedge of lemon, bay leaf, parsley, thyme, peppercorns, onion and carrot. Cover with water to a depth of about 1.5"/4cm, bring to the boil, cover and simmer for 3 minutes. Add the trout, replace the lid and poach gently for 5 minutes. Remove the pan from the heat and allow fish to cool in the stock.

To make the sauce, peel and finely dice the cucumber. Cover with a plate and leave to stand for 15-20 minutes. Drain off excess water. Stir the diced cucumber into the yoghurt.

Remove the trout from the liquid when quite cold and arrange on a serving dish. Garnish with lemon wedges and serve the cucumber sauce separately.

FRIED TROUT AND CUCUMBER
(serves 4)

4 trout (gutted, cleaned and patted dry)
1 dessertspoon flour seasoned with salt & pepper
4oz/100g butter
1 cucumber (peeled and cut into 2"/5cm lengths)
1 lemon (cut into wedges)

Boil the cucumber in lightly salted water until almost tender. Drain and set aside.
Roll the trout in seasoned flour. Put the butter in a large frying pan and melt until
hot. Fry the trout gently for about 12-15 minutes, turning carefully and basting.
Drain and put on a warmed serving dish and keep heated. Put the cucumber in the
pan in which the fish was fried and cook gently for 5 minutes. Arrange cucumber
around the fish and serve immediately with wedges of lemon.

Normandy Trout
(serves 4)

4 trout (washed and dried)
1 tablespoon/15ml water
Juice of 1 lemon
Salt & pepper
Chopped chives and parsley
3fl.oz/75ml double cream
1oz/25g white breadcrumbs
A little melted butter

Set oven at 180C/350F/Gas Mark 4.

Lay the trout in a well-buttered fireproof dish, add the spoonful of water, lemon juice, salt and pepper and the chives and parsley. Cook for 10-15 minutes. While fish is cooking put the cream in a small saucepan and boil for a minute or two. Pour over the cooked trout, sprinkle over the breadcrumbs and then the melted butter and brown under a grill. Serve immediately.

STOCKS AND SAUCES FOR FISH DISHES

COURT BOUILLON

2 pints/1.2litres water or water and wine
3oz/75g chopped onion
1 medium carrot (sliced)
1 garlic clove (finely chopped)
1 celery stalk (finely sliced)
1 sprig each of parsley and thyme
1 bayleaf
1 clove
2 teaspoon salt
4 peppercorns

Put all the ingredients in a large pan, cover and simmer for 30 minutes. Strain, cover and refrigerate for up to 3 days. Use for poaching or boiling fish.

NB. If you are poaching a large salmon you will need to increase the above quantities.

BASIC FISH STOCK
(to make 4 pints/2 litres)

4-5lb/1.8-2.2kg of fish bones and trimmings
4oz/125g sliced onions
1oz/25g parsley stalks
10fl.ozs/250ml white wine
Juice of 1 lemon
4 pints/2000ml water
12 white peppercorns

Put all the ingredients in a large pan, except for the peppercorns. Bring the mixture to the boil, skim and leave to simmer slowly for 20 minutes. Add the peppercorns and cook for a further 10 minutes. Remove from heat and pass stock through a fine sieve. Retain the fish stock to use where needed with your fish dishes. Will keep in a covered container in a refrigerator for up to 3 days.

BEURRE MANIÉ

4oz/100g butter (softened)
3oz/75g flour

Knead butter and flour together thoroughly and use for thickening sauces, vegetables, etc.

BASIC WHITE SAUCE FOR FISH DISHES
(sufficient for 4)

1oz/25g butter
1oz/25g plain flour
10fl.ozs/275ml milk★
Salt and white pepper

★You may prefer to substitute equal quantities of milk and fish stock to make the same amount or just use fish stock.

In a small pan melt the butter over a low heat, stir in the flour and cook for one minute. Remove from heat. Stirring constantly, add the milk and/or stock and return pan to the heat. Bring to the boil and simmer very gently for about 5 minutes until sauce is smooth and creamy. Add salt and pepper to taste.

Parsley Sauce – Add two tablespoons chopped fresh parsley to the sauce.

Hot Tartare Sauce – Add 1 teaspoon chopped fresh parsley, 1 teaspoon finely chopped onion, 3 finely chopped pickled gherkins and 12 chopped capers to the sauce.

BEARNAISE SAUCE

1¹/₂ teaspoons of finely chopped shallots
3.5fl.oz/80ml white wine
1fl.oz/25ml tarragon vinegar
1oz/25g chopped tarragon
2 teaspoons chopped chervil
Pinch white pepper
Pinch of salt
3 egg yolks
10oz/250g melted butter
Half teaspoon chopped tarragon
Half teaspoon chopped chervil

Put the shallots, white wine, tarragon vinegar, chopped tarragon and chervil, and pepper in a pan, bring to the boil and reduce by about half. Allow mixture to cool and transfer to a bowl. Add the egg yolks and salt, put the bowl in a pan of water and heat slowly, stirring constantly, until the yolks thicken. Gradually add the melted butter, ensuring the mixture does not over-heat. The sauce should now be smooth. Adjust seasoning to taste and then pass sauce through a fine sieve or muslin. Add the remaining tarragon and chervil and gently warm before serving.

HOLLANDAISE SAUCE
(serves 4)

3 egg yolks
1 tablespoon/15ml lemon juice
1 tablespoon/15ml warm water
Salt & white pepper
4oz/100g unsalted butter (melted)

Put the egg yolks, lemon juice and water in a liquidizer or food processor and whiz. Add the salt and pepper. Gradually pour in the melted butter through the funnel while mixer is running slowly until all is thoroughly blended and the sauce thickened. Adjust seasoning to taste and serve warmed.

MAYONNAISE
(sufficient for 4-6)

1 egg and 1 egg yolk
Half teaspoon mustard powder
Salt and white pepper
10fl.ozs/275ml olive oil
1 tablespoon/15ml wine vinegar or lemon juice

Put the egg, egg yolk, mustard, salt and pepper in a food processor and whiz. With the processor running slowly add and oil through the feeder tube and process until mixture thickens. Add the vinegar or lemon juice.

MOUSSELINE SAUCE
(serves 4)

Make basic sauce as for Hollandaise Sauce (see page 109) and fold in 6fl.oz/150ml of whipped cream. Serve sauce warm with cold fish dish.

SAUCE VERTE
(serves 4-6)

1oz/25g spinach leaves
1oz/25g watercress (with stalks removed)
2oz/50g parsley, chervil and tarragon in equal quantities
20fl.oz/500ml mayonnaise
Salt & pepper

Blanch the spinach, watercress and herbs, allow to cool and pass through a fine sieve. Add 2 tablespoons/30ml of mayonnaise and mix into a purée. Add purée to the remaining mayonnaise, season with salt and pepper to taste and serve.

TARTARE SAUCE - RECIPE 1

Mix as for mayonnaise and then fold in 1 teaspoon chopped fresh parsley, 1 teaspoon finely chopped onion, 3 finely chopped pickled gherkins and 12 chopped capers.

TARTARE SAUCE - RECIPE 2
(sufficient for 6)

2 egg yolks
Half teaspoon seal
Quarter teaspoon freshly ground black pepper
Half teaspoon sugar
6fl.oz/150ml olive oil
3 tablespoons/45ml wine vinegar
1 teaspoon Dijon mustard
1 teaspoon chopped gherkins
1 teaspoon chopped capers
1 tablespoon chopped parsley and chives
1 hard-boiled egg (finely chopped)

Put the egg yolks into a liquidizer or food processor with the salt, pepper and sugar and whiz. Gradually add the oil through the feeder until it is all absorbed and then add the vinegar and mustard. Pour mixture into a bowl and stir in the gherkins, capers, herbs and the hard-boiled egg. If desired, add a few stoned finely chopped black olives.